21ST CENTURY DEBATES

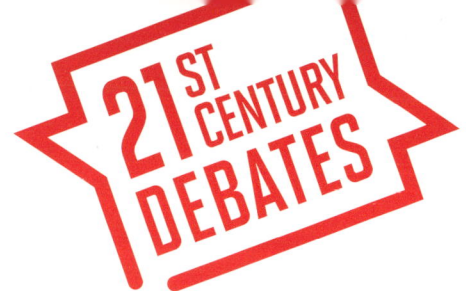

HOW TO DEAL WITH

# Drug Wars

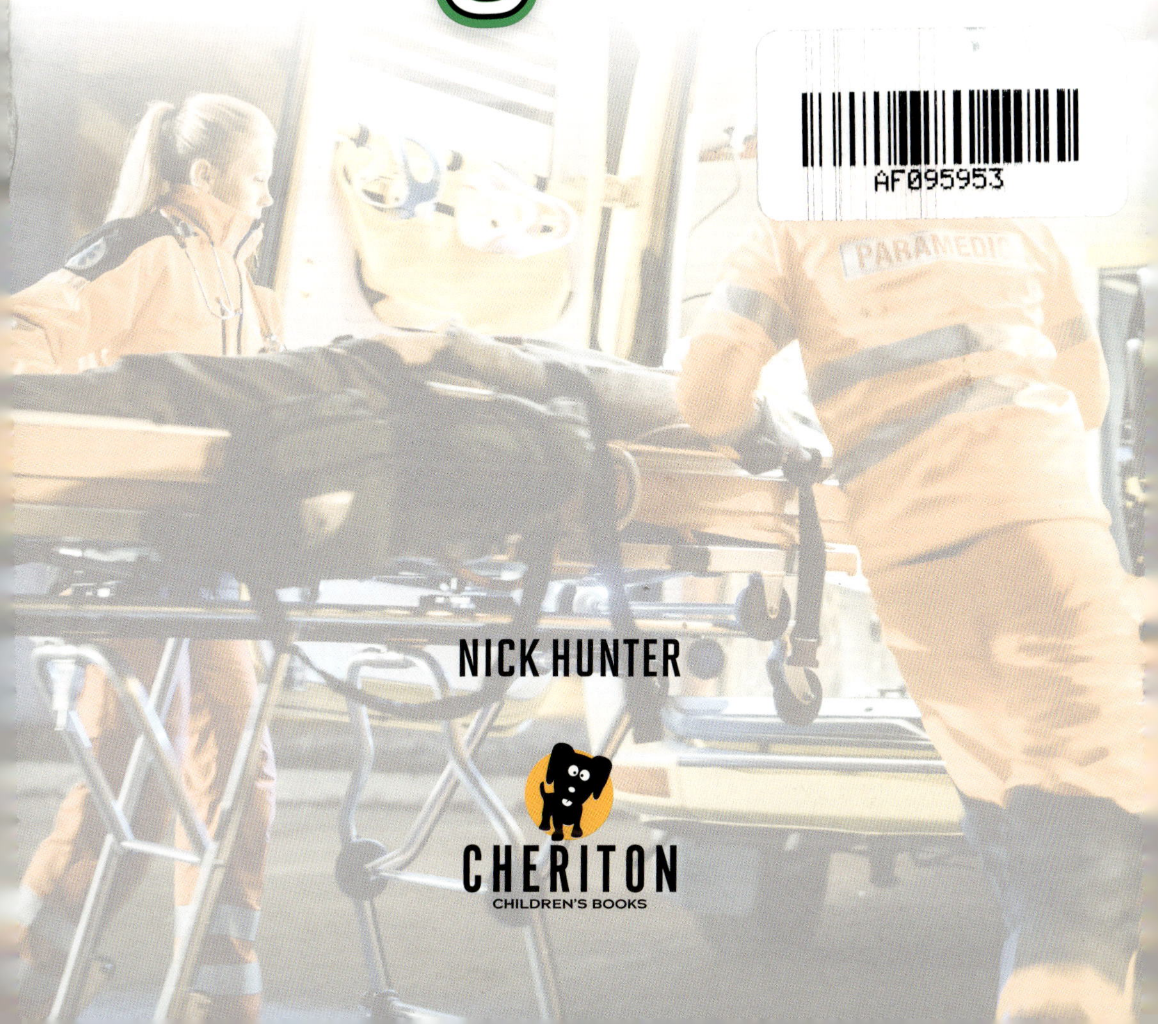



NICK HUNTER

CHERITON
CHILDREN'S BOOKS

Published in 2026 by **Cheriton Children's Books**
1 Bank Drive West, Shrewsbury, Shropshire, SY3 9DJ, UK

© Copyright 2026 Cheriton Children's Books

First Edition

Author: Nick Hunter
Designer: Paul Myerscough
Editor: Sarah Eason
Proofreader: Nicky Hughes

Picture credits: Cover: Shutterstock/Octavio Hoyos.
Inside: p1: Shutterstock/Gorodenkoff, p4: Shutterstock/
Ground Picture, p5: Shutterstock/Nomad Soul, p6: Shutterstock/
Mr Yanukit, p7: Shutterstock/Ratuay, p8: Shutterstock/Leon Rafael,
p9: Shutterstock/279photo Studio, p10: Shutterstock/Roberto Galan,
p12: Shutterstock/Images By Kenny, p13: Wikimedia Commons/US
National Archives and Records Administration, p14: Shutterstock/
David Huamani Bedoya, p15: Shutterstock/Pressmaster, p16:
Shutterstock/PeopleImages.com/Yuri A, p18: Shutterstock/Tero
Vesalainen, p19: Shutterstock/Goami, p20: Shutterstock/Virrage
Images, p21: Shutterstock/Phil Pasquini, p22: Shutterstock/
van Blerk, p23: Shutterstock/Rblfmr, p24: Shutterstock/Gorodenkoff,
p26: Shutterstock/Ann Kosolapova, p27: Shutterstock/Rebekah
Zemansky, p28: Shutterstock/Kristi Blokhin, p29: Shutterstock/
Gorodenkoff, p30: Shutterstock/Roberto Galan, p31: Shutterstock/
Chris Harwood, p32: Shutterstock/Drazen Zigic, p34: Shutterstock/
Phil Pasquini, p35: Shutterstock/Adam Melnyk, p36: Shutterstock/
Belish, p37: Shutterstock, p38: Shutterstock/David Huamani Bedoya,
p40: Shutterstock/Phil Pasquini, p41: Shutterstock/King Ropes Access,
p42: Shutterstock/Frontpage, p44: Shutterstock/Phil Pasquini.

All rights reserved. No part of this book may be reproduced in any
form without permission of the publisher, except by a reviewer.

Printed in China

Please visit our website,
www.cheritonchildrensbooks.com
to see more of our high-quality books.

# Contents

Introduction
**The War on Drugs** .................................. 4

Chapter 1
**What Are Drug Wars?** .............................. 6

Chapter 2
**Why Do Drug Wars Happen?** ..................... 12

Chapter 3
**Living with Drug Wars** ............................ 18

Chapter 4
**Drug Wars and Society** ........................... 26

Chapter 5
**Tackling Drug Wars** ............................... 34

Chapter 6
**Solutions to Drug Wars** .......................... 40

Find Out More .......................................... 45
Glossary ................................................. 46
Index and About the Author ......................... 48

Introduction
# The War on Drugs

The war on drugs promised strong penalties for selling, buying, and using drugs.

In July 1971, President Richard Nixon announced that the United States was declaring war. The war being waged was not against any country or army. Instead, it was against the smuggling, supply, and use of illegal drugs. Nixon described drug abuse as "public enemy number one." Later presidents and lawmakers have followed him in setting aside huge resources to fight the growing problem of drug use and addiction.

## The Longest War

The war on drugs has been fought by police and criminal gangs on the streets of US cities. It has also been fought against those bringing illegal drugs into the United States in Mexico and Central America. Powerful drug cartels and communities grow and process drugs in countries such as Colombia, in South America, and Afghanistan, in Central Asia. The cartels have also been targeted as US authorities try to stop the flow of drugs to the United States.

More than 50 years later, there is still no sign of a victory in the war on drugs. Illegal drug use continues to have a big impact on individuals and society across the nation. In 2023 alone, more than 100,000 people died from drug overdoses in the United States.

Many more lives were affected by drug-related crime and social issues. The war has changed as powerful synthetic opioid drugs have become a bigger problem in recent decades.

## Cost of War

Experts believe that the government has spent more than $1 trillion in pursuing the war on drugs since 1971, with billions of dollars spent every year. In spite of this, the majority of Americans still believe that the drug problem in the United States is extremely serious. There is a human cost too. As well as the health effects, many thousands of people are in prison for drug-related crimes.

## How Can This War Be Won?

The continuing problem of illegal drug use has led many people to question whether the war on drugs has been worthwhile. What is needed to win the war, and does the approach to the entire problem of drug wars need to change completely?

### A Twenty-First Century Debate

There are many questions about continuing drug wars, how drugs impact people's lives, and the best ways of dealing with this issue. People have differing views about this twenty-first century problem. This book looks at the facts about drugs and drug wars. It also explores some of the debates that surround drug wars and their effect on both individuals and society.

Billions of dollars are spent each year policing illegal drugs.

Chapter 1

# What Are Drug Wars?

The use of drugs has many negative health effects and leads to social problems, such as crime and violence related to the supply of drugs. The damage caused by the use of illegal drugs means that the United States and many other countries have made a huge effort to stop this trade by declaring war on drugs. However, this war has negative consequences of its own.

## The Drug Problem

A drug is any chemical or natural substance, other than food, that produces a biological effect in the body or the brain. Not all drugs are illegal: We use drugs as medicines to cure illness and relieve pain. Adults are also allowed to use drugs such as alcohol. Some drugs are classed as illegal substances because they have health risks. These risks include addiction—when someone is unable to stop taking the drug. This may affect their ability to do normal things such as work or care for others. Addiction can also lead to crime because addicts need to find money to buy the drugs they need to feed their addiction.

Marijuana and cannabis are made from hemp plants.

*Opium plants grow in Asian countries such as Myanmar.*

## Drug Dangers

Addiction and use of illegal drugs can also have a long-term impact on users' mental health. Other health issues include the risk of driving while under the influence of drugs, which could endanger the driver and other people. When people inject drugs, this can spread infectious diseases such as HIV.

Harmful illegal drugs are grouped into different categories, such as these:

- Opioid drugs are substances that are based on the opium poppy, or synthetic drugs that have similar effects. Opioid drugs are used to produce legal painkillers as well as illegal drugs such as heroin. The illegal use of opioids is the cause of many deaths from overdose. This has grown in recent years because of the use of powerful synthetic opioids such as fentanyl.
- Cocaine is made from the leaves of the coca plant, often grown in South America. Cocaine is addictive and deaths often result from the drug being mixed with other substances, including opioids.
- Methamphetamine is also known as Crystal Meth. It is extremely addictive and can cause a number of serious health issues. They include anxiety, mood problems, and violent behavior.
- Marijuana and cannabis are made from the leaves and other parts of the hemp plant, and include the mind-altering substance THC. Use of marijuana can have long-term mental and physical effects. It is seen as less dangerous than some other drugs and use of it is legal in some states.

## An Illegal Industry

The global production and trade in illegal drugs is a huge industry, even though the products of that industry are banned in most countries. One estimate claims that drug users in the United States spend more than $100 billion every year on illegal drugs. That figure does not include the illegal use of prescription drugs.

Illegal drugs are often grown or produced outside the United States. There is also a large trade from drug-producing countries in Asia and South America to other parts of the world, such as Europe. Synthetic drugs are a growing problem. The sums of money that drug producers and traffickers can earn from this deadly trade are enormous.

## A War on Drug Supply

The US Government and other countries launched a war on drugs to tackle this huge industry and the impact of illegal drugs on American citizens and society. It involves many different elements. In the United States, the war on drugs has led to tough penalties and prison sentences for possession and supply of drugs. In addition, there is also a focus on working with other countries to reduce the supply of drugs. That is done by targeting and disrupting international drug smuggling. There are also attempts to stop drug production in countries such as Afghanistan, where much of the world's supply of heroin originates.

The profits from trading illegal drugs are so great that people are willing to commit violent acts to continue to benefit from the trade.

These policemen in Afghanistan are destroying a field of opium plants. However, measures such as this often have little long-lasting effect on the drug trade.

## International Drug Wars

Because supply of illegal drugs is such a big business, efforts to stop the supply will often result in conflict with heavily armed and violent drug gangs. Another form of drug war is the constant struggle between the different crime organizations linked to the drug trade. Attempts by governments to stop the drug trade through Central America to the United States have been matched by the huge growth of heavily armed organized crime gangs and a massive increase in homicide in many places across the region.

## Leading to Gang Wars

As governments have waged a war to control the supply and use of drugs, this has led to gang warfare in many parts of the world and on the streets of American cities. These smaller-scale conflicts between criminal gangs to control the supply of drugs in American cities and states also claim many lives. All of these different conflicts can be seen as drug wars. Unfortunately, peace is still a long way away in the global struggle over drugs.

# 21ST CENTURY DEBATES

# Can Any Single Country Stop the Supply of Illegal Drugs?

The supply and use of drugs is a global problem. Drugs are farmed and produced in countries that are often far from the places where demand for illegal drugs is highest. Those places include the United States and Europe. Given this global trade, many people argue that it is impossible for any single country to control illegal drug use. Others say it is essential that individual countries find a way to control the supply and use of illegal drugs. Let's take a look at the two arguments.

## The Supply of Drugs Can Never Be Stopped

Many people argue that it is impossible for one country to deal with the supply of illegal drugs for the following reasons:

**Demand drives supply:** If people want something, this is called demand. Demand for illegal drugs is high because many people want them or are addicted to them. For that reason, it is very difficult to stop the supply to meet the demand.

**International networks:** Drugs pass through many different stages between the farming of raw materials to being sold and consumed on the streets of American cities. It is very difficult for one country, however powerful it is, to break up such complex and far-reaching networks.

**Advantages of traffickers:** Drug producers and smugglers have advantages over governments. They can be flexible and they do not follow the law. If some drugs are discovered before they reach their destination, this is often just a small part of the total supply.

## Conclusion

The global drug trade is incredibly wide-reaching and complex. That makes it very difficult for any one country to stop drugs reaching their destination. Governments may have some success, but drugs will always get through somehow.

## Targeting Drug Supply Can Work

Supporters of attempts to stop drugs before they reach users argue this can work for these reasons:

**Cutting demand:** Stopping supply of drugs could be combined with measures to cut demand. They include campaigns to warn about risks of drugs and medical support for those suffering addiction.

**Controlling borders:** Government may not be able to control what happens on another continent. However, they should be able to stop drugs and other illegal goods from crossing our borders.

**International effort:** The war on drugs is not one country against the world. Many countries want to stop the supply of drugs and the problems they cause. If countries work together, this is achievable.

## Conclusion

Trying to stop the supply of drugs is just one of many different measures that can be taken to try to control drugs. Our government can also work with other countries, including those where the drugs are produced. If they tighten up border controls, it will make life more difficult for traffickers. Those combined factors will help us win the war on drugs.

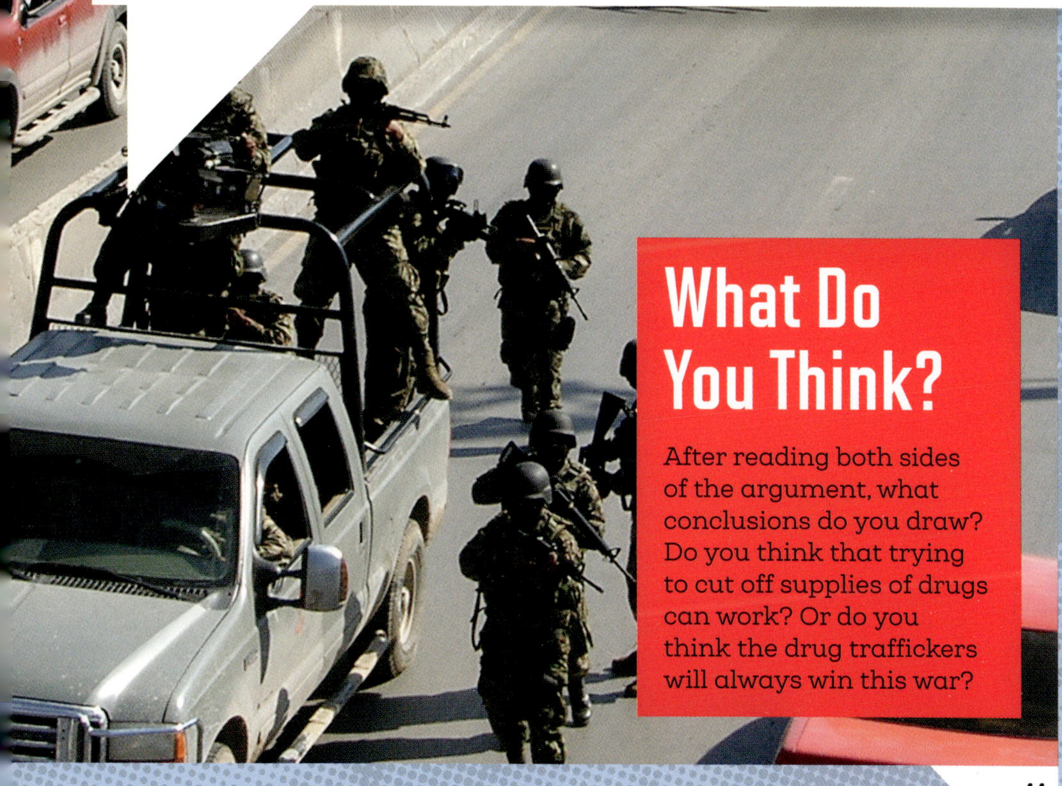

## What Do You Think?

After reading both sides of the argument, what conclusions do you draw? Do you think that trying to cut off supplies of drugs can work? Or do you think the drug traffickers will always win this war?

Chapter 2

# Why Do Drug Wars Happen?

Penalties for highly addictive crack cocaine have traditionally been higher than for similar amounts of other drugs.

Drug wars are a result of a combination of different forces. Governments try to control what drugs people can use because of health issues and other concerns, such as whether people will be able to work. But it is very difficult to stop supply completely, and addiction increases demand for illegal drugs. Drug traffickers and suppliers can make a lot of money from the trade, so they are prepared to risk getting caught up in a drug war.

## A Crusade Begins

Until the early 1900s there were few restrictions on the use of drugs. In 1914, the Harrison Act was the first Federal law to regulate and tax the use of cocaine and opium-based drugs. In 1937, a Marijuana Act put taxes on the sale of marijuana, but the drug was not banned. The Controlled Substances Act of 1970 restricted the sale and use of many substances on the basis that they were deemed harmful to public health.

## Nixon's War

When President Nixon announced a war on drugs shortly after 1970, he increased funding for drug enforcement. That helped with setting up the Drug Enforcement Administration (DEA) in 1973, and introducing stricter sentencing for drug crimes. However, Nixon's opponents believed this was designed to attack particular groups of people. They were young people who opposed the Vietnam War, and Black Americans.

President Richard Nixon launched the war on drugs.

## Tough Laws

Later, during the 1980s, President Reagan introduced mandatory prison sentences for possession of some drugs. These tougher laws were driven by public concern about the growth in use of crack cocaine and the social issues and crime that came with it. Many people believed that the laws unfairly affected the Black community. That was because the laws imposed tougher sentences for drugs that were more common in Black neighborhoods. The laws led to a large increase in the number of people who were imprisoned for drug crimes, particularly Black Americans. In 1980, there were 50,000 people in prison for nonviolent drug offenses. By 1997, this number had increased to 400,000 people.

## Lack of Success?

As the government imposed harsher penalties for drug users, the number of people using drugs declined in the early years of the war on drugs. However, since then, drug use has increased and the resulting health issues have continued to rise. Drug-related deaths in the United States rose from just over one per 100,000 people in 1980 to 19 per 100,000 people in 2021. That is much higher than the drug-related deaths in other countries that are similar to the United States. One big reason for the surge in overdoses is the growth of synthetic opioid drugs. Often these drugs were prescribed by doctors. They also found their way into the illegal market, where there are no controls on how people use them.

## Reducing Crime

One of the key reasons for the government's campaign against illegal drugs was to bring communities together. The hope was that it would reduce crime and other issues associated with drug abuse. However, many campaigners argue that the war on drugs has failed to achieve this.

The problem is that more public information about drugs and harsher sentences have not been successful in reducing demand for these illegal substances. This is partly because many drugs are addictive, so users are prepared to break the law because of their need for the drugs. Where there is demand for something, there will likely be someone who is prepared to take the risk to meet that demand. This is even true when the prices for drugs increase because of government attempts to stop the trade.

## Criminal Networks

As a result of the demand for drugs, a network of criminal gangs has grown to supply the substances. These gangs recruit young people to sell drugs, who are often from the country's poorest neighborhoods, where there are few other opportunities for jobs and status. The gangs use violence to stop other gangs moving on to their turf. Many of the junior dealers end up in prison. They also become victims of gun violence as drug wars spill on to the streets of US cities.

Drug wars often touch the lives of people who live far from the United States. In countries like Peru, the military is involved in trying to stop farming of the coca plant that is refined to produce cocaine. Poor families and children may be employed on these farms.

Criminal gangs make large profits from supplying drugs, which can then be used to fund other businesses.

## International Drug Wars

The health and social effects of the drugs trade are not a concern for the producers and traffickers supplying illegal drugs around the world. They can earn huge rewards from providing illegal drugs to users in the United States and elsewhere. The efforts to stop this supply lead to conflict between governments and drug cartels in many countries. They also cause battles between the different drug producers. In 2006, Mexico launched a military war on cartels. Since then, the country has seen more than 400,000 homicides. Many of the countries with the world's highest homicide rates lie in Central America and the Caribbean. Both areas sit directly on the drug-trafficking routes to the United States.

### Drugonomics

One reason why drug producers are prepared to fight drug wars is the amount of money that can be made. Cocaine is sold to users in the United States for more than 150 times what it costs to produce. These massive profits enable drug cartels to pay for private armies to protect their trade.

# 21ST CENTURY DEBATES

## Is Treating Addicts More Effective than Stopping Drugs?

Many experts argue that the United States' war on drugs has been ineffective in reducing the supply of drugs into the country and the number of health issues associated with drugs. Drug treatment has been part of this war, but often only after drug users are in prison. Would the drive to cut use of illegal drugs be more effective if there was more focus on helping drug users to deal with addiction? Some people are strongly in favor of this, but others disagree. Let's take a look at both sides of the debate.

## Make Drug Treatment Available to All

Experts who argue that the war on drugs has failed support more treatment for addicts for the following reasons:

**Reduce demand:** Previous attempts to cut drug use have failed because they are not dealing with the great demand for drugs that comes from addiction. Treating people who want to quit drugs will cut the demand.

**Keep drug users out of prison:** Sending people to prison for possessing or using illegal drugs is not addressing the causes of the problem. It is very expensive and is unlikely to help people quit drugs. It may lead to more serious crimes because convicted drug users may not be able to find other work when their prison sentence ends.

**Cutting crime and violence:** Drug addiction often leads to other crimes such as robbery to fund drugs. Treating addicts as a first step will reduce the crime and social problems associated with drugs.

## Conclusion

Treatment for drug addicts will deal with the use of illegal drugs as a health issue rather than a crime. People will be able to receive treatment and then get on with their lives rather than spending time in prison. Reducing the prison population will save money, which can then be used to pay for the cost of treatment for drug addicts.

## Treatment Does Not Work

Opponents of offering treatment to drug addicts argue that it is the wrong approach to tackling drugs for the following reasons:

**Crimes should be punished:** Drug addicts are responsible for crime and social problems because of the choices they make. Treatment may be effective for many drug abusers, but we still expect people to be punished for breaking the law.

**Prison deters crime:** Prison is a deterrent that stops people committing crime. If people know they will just be given treatment, what reason do they have to stop taking drugs in the first place?

**Treatment will not stop supply of drugs:** If people do not want to quit drugs, treatment is unlikely to make any difference to them. The supply of drugs needs to be tackled as well as treatment to stop people becoming addicts.

## Conclusion

It would be easy to think that the crime and violence associated with drugs could be fixed by treating drug users rather than enforcing the law, but will this really work? It will not deter people from taking drugs and will not cure people unless they want to quit drugs.

## What Do You Think?

After reading both sides of the argument, what conclusions do you draw? Do you think treating drug addicts would be more effective than the current war on drugs? Or do you think this approach would not be tough enough?

Chapter 3

# Living with Drug Wars

Many experts think that dealing with drug addiction is the best way to stop people using drugs.

For many people and communities, the effects of drug use and drug wars are a daily reality that they would like to escape. Drug users have to deal with addiction and other health risks. They also have to deal with the long-term effects of their addiction, such as poverty or unemployment. These problems have a knock-on effect on the lives of family and friends. The criminal networks involved in trafficking drugs have an impact on the whole community. And the effects of the war on drugs spread around the world.

## Health Effects

One effect of the war on drugs was to group all illegal drugs together. In fact, the effect of some drugs is much greater than others. Illegal drugs cause the release of a substance called dopamine in our brains, that leads to a feeling of pleasure. Taking drugs can change the way the brain works. That makes it difficult to make good choices. It also leads to an intense craving or need for more of the drug. This is called addiction or dependency. Addiction can also lead to other health problems, including heart and liver damage.

## Death from Drugs

Illegal drug use is a major cause of death. It can result either from an overdose, long-term effects of drug-taking, or a related illness. Overdose is a particular problem associated with opioid drugs such as heroin and synthetic opioids including fentanyl. When a drug user overdoses, the amount of the drug in their body means that the person becomes unresponsive and stops breathing. The spread of synthetic opioids has been linked to a large increase in deaths due to drug overdose in the United States.

The way drugs are used can also have an impact. Different drugs are consumed in a variety of ways. Some users inject drugs into their bloodstream, but this may be done with dirty or shared needles that can cause serious infections. Dirty needles can also pass on infectious diseases such as HIV and hepatitis B and C, which affect the liver.

## Unknown Risks

Some of the most serious effects come from the illegal nature of drugs. That means there is no control over the harmful chemicals that illegal drugs may contain or be mixed with. For example, if you buy a packet of painkillers in a pharmacy, you know what it contains. However, there is no guarantee for those who use illegal drugs. This can make it difficult to be sure about the effects and health risks to the user.

The health effects of using dirty syringes can be worse than the health problems caused by the drugs themselves.

## Changing Lives of Users

Drug addiction can damage a user's health, but it can also make other areas of life difficult. The need to find and use more illegal drugs affects an addict's everyday life. This may make it difficult to work and keep a regular job. Addicts are also at greater risk of family breakup and possibly becoming homeless. Drug addiction is an issue for many homeless people. Addicts can also find themselves in dangerous situations when buying drugs. Many addicts turn to crime to find money to fund their addiction. And as a result, they run the risk of being arrested and sent to prison.

## Changing Lives of Friends and Family

When someone has an addiction, it does not just change their life but also the lives of their family and friends. Drug users can behave unpredictably. They may be violent or difficult to deal with. Their constant focus on drugs and money to support their addiction can also cause issues, such as stealing from others or being unable to pay bills.

## Affecting Communities

Drug-related crime also affects the wider community. Robberies from people and property are often linked to drug addiction. Addiction also changes the way a person behaves and can cause them to commit crime. That is because they are not in control of their mind or body.

Drug addiction is a major cause of crimes such as robbery.

The opioid crisis has affected communities across the country and caused tragic deaths in many families.

## The Opioid Crisis

Since 2000, a new drug crisis has hit the United States. It began with the prescribing of legal pain relief made from powerful synthetic opioids. These legal opioids were marketed as effective painkillers but were also highly addictive. In order to feed their addiction, people turned to illegal supplies of synthetic opioids such as fentanyl. This opioid crisis has been responsible for the sharp rise in numbers of deaths from overdose in the United States, which are now much higher than in other countries.

### How Common Is Drug Addiction?

Around one in 100 of the global population is dependent on illegal drugs. Figures for the United States are higher than this average, with 3.8 percent of people having a drug dependency. This figure has almost doubled since 1990 because of the opioid crisis that is affecting the nation. In Canada, 2.3 percent of people are dependent on illegal drugs. Many people are also dependent on legal drugs such as alcohol and tobacco, which also cause serious health problems.

Drug abuse is a major cause of homelessness.

## Caught in Drug Wars

Drug addiction clearly has negative effects on addicts and those around them. However, the war on drugs also impacts the lives of individuals. Many experts dispute whether the tougher sentences for drug use actually stop people from taking drugs. Studies have found that other factors may be more important in determining whether people use illegal drugs.

Drug users are more likely to come from poorer and more vulnerable groups in society. They may already be struggling with issues that lead to drug use, such as unemployment, bad housing, or poor health. For example, users of synthetic opioids may have started using the drugs legally because of a health issue. They then became sucked into illegal drug use when they found themselves dependent on the drugs. Treating drug use as a crime rather than a health issue does not help these people deal with their problems. For example, having spent time in prison, drug users may then be unable to find housing or a steady job.

## Drug-Related Violence

Drug wars and drug-related crime have more impact in some communities than others. In the next chapter we will see that many experts feel drug wars are a big contributor to racial inequality across the United States. Drug trafficking is linked to gang culture in many areas. These same gangs are also responsible for high levels of gun violence and homicide. However, there are also other social problems leading to gang culture. They include high unemployment and poor education, which means that young men have few other opportunities in life.

Communities involved in drug production and trafficking around the world have also been affected by higher levels of crime. Many of those killed in battles between drug cartels are innocent people caught up in this violence.

## Has the War on Drugs Made Things Worse?

Opponents of the war on drugs say it has not helped many of the people affected by drug use and drug-related crime, even if some people are deterred from taking illegal drugs. They argue that the hardline approach to dealing with drug users makes it much more difficult to protect public health. Opponents of the war on drugs believe that supporting drug users is more effective. That includes providing drug users with clean syringes for injecting, which reduces the spread of diseases such as HIV. Police crackdowns can also lead to more violence as drug traffickers try to match the force used by the authorities. This increases gun-related crime, so drug wars spread even farther across the community.

Protesters in New York City calling for marijuana to be legal.

# 21ST CENTURY DEBATES

## Is Drug Violence More Damaging than Drugs?

The criminal networks that supply illegal drugs have a wider impact on communities across the United States. They recruit gang members to control the supply of drugs, and take part in other criminal activities. Some people argue that the crime and violence related to drug trafficking causes as much damage and misery as the drugs themselves. Others believe that tight control is needed to stop the activity of criminal networks. Let's take a look at both sides of the debate.

## Drugs Are the Main Problem

People argue that drugs are the main issue we need to deal with for the following reasons:

**Overdoses and health effects:** More than 100,000 people die every year from overdoses in the United States, many caused by the spread of opioid drugs. This is around four times the number of people who die from gun homicides. Illegal drugs also have many other negative health effects.

**Effects on family:** Drug use and addiction damages the lives of the drug user's family and friends. It can lead to other issues such as unemployment, homelessness, and family breakup.

**Effects of hardline war on drugs:** Experts believe tough prison terms for drug users have failed to stop the spread of illegal drugs. The sentences have also been very damaging to people incarcerated for just minor offenses.

## Conclusion

The number of people dying from drug overdoses is just one of the negative effects of illegal drug use. Drug use and attempts to stop people using illegal drugs cause huge damage to families and also impact the wider community.

## Drug-Related Violence Is More Harmful than Drugs

Those who argue that criminal networks and gun violence around drugs do most harm give the following reasons:

**Gun homicides:** Many of the thousands of gun homicides and injuries in the United States are linked to gangs and arguments about drug supply. Some people believe that decriminalizing drugs would make it easier to deal with dangerous criminal gangs.

**Effects of gun violence:** Most of the violence related to drugs takes place in poorer neighborhoods and so has the greatest effect on Black Americans and other people of color. This violence damages the whole neighborhood because it means there are fewer businesses and good jobs in these areas.

**Global impact:** Many of the countries with the highest homicide rates in the world are on drug trafficking routes into the United States, and these areas often face armed conflict to end drug trafficking. Many innocent people are dying because of the illegal drug trade.

## Conclusion

The illegal drug trade and the attempts to stop it are violent and destructive. Thousands of people are caught up in this violence and its far-reaching effects. It is impossible to separate this impact from the illegal drug trade itself.

## What Do You Think?

After reading both sides of the argument, what conclusions do you draw? Do you think stopping people from using illegal drugs should be the main focus of the war on drugs? Or do you think ending drug-related violence is even more important?

# Chapter 4
# Drug Wars and Society

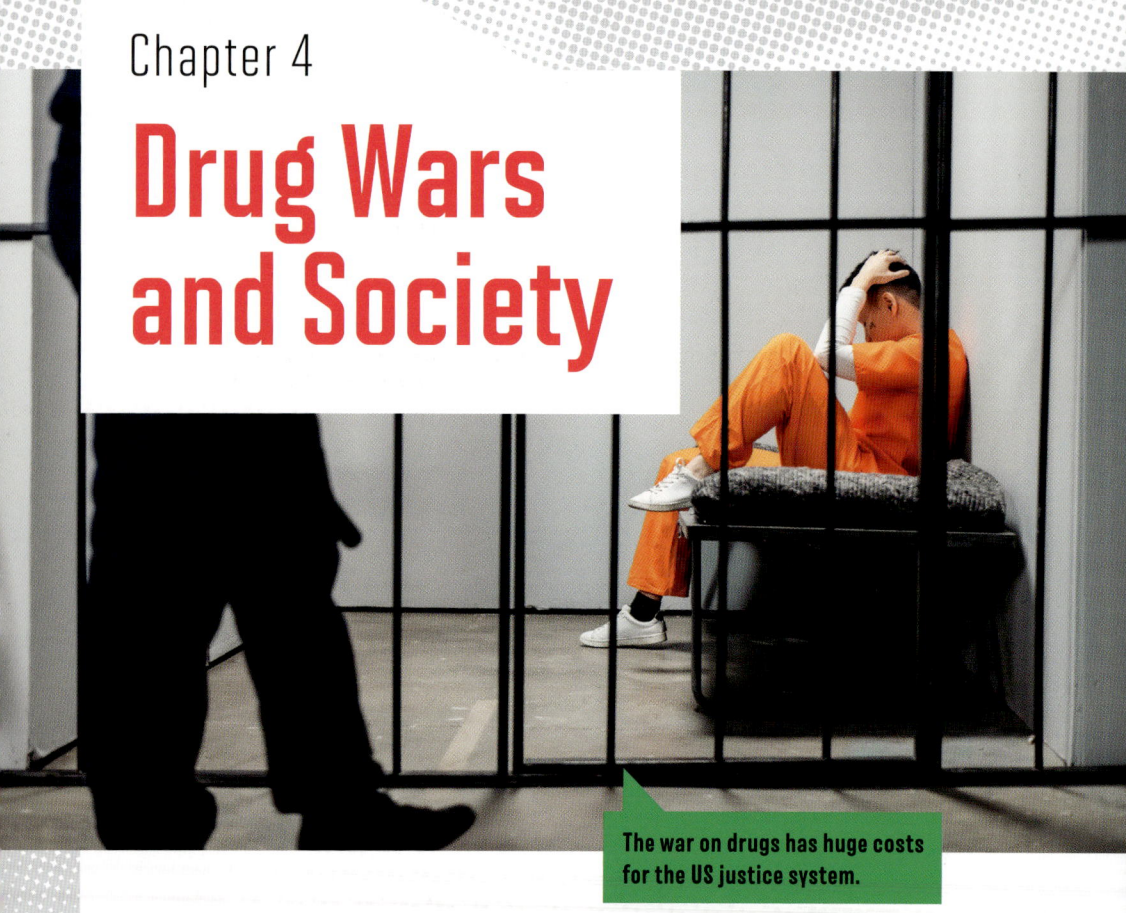

The war on drugs has huge costs for the US justice system.

Drug wars can have a devastating impact on the lives of individual drug users and the people around them, but issues around drugs also have an impact across our society. The ongoing cost of the government's war on drugs falls on all of us, and this war has a greater impact on some communities. Drugs and drug wars affect other areas of our system too, such as healthcare and the justice system. The global trade in drugs also damages societies far beyond the borders of the United States.

## Harming Society

We have already seen that the war on drugs that the US Government has fought since the 1970s has failed to stop the flow of drugs into our society. Drug dependency and deaths from overdoses are higher in the United States than almost any other country in the world. Of course, these drug problems could have been even worse without the war on drugs. What effect has this difficult battle had on society as a whole?

## Prison Problems

One of the main effects of the war on drugs in the United States is the focus on tougher penalties and mandatory prison sentences for drug possession and other nonviolent offenses. This has overloaded courts and prison systems dealing with what many people see as minor offenders. Keeping someone in prison costs tens of thousands of dollars every year. During their sentence, these people are not working and are therefore not paying taxes. That hits the wider economy and puts a big burden on taxpayers.

Historically, a high number of drug arrests have been for possession of marijuana. Many states have decided to decriminalize possession of this drug. That is partly because of the high cost and effects of prosecuting users.

Critics of the war on drugs say that focus on convicting minor offenders is draining police resources. That means the police are failing to put enough time and money into dealing with the crime organizations that have become rich and powerful because of the addictions of ordinary Americans. These crime organizations are also involved in other criminal areas, such as people trafficking and violent crime, such as murder.

### Prison Crisis

The US Federal Bureau of Prisons (BOP) calculates that 44 percent of the federal prison population is locked up because of offenses involving drugs. Thirteen percent of these offenders committed nonviolent crimes.

It can be difficult for drug offenders to rebuild their lives after even a short time in prison.

Racial inequality between white Americans and people of color is made worse by the effects of the war on drugs.

## The Economic Cost

The government's war on drugs has a high cost in police time and resources. However, there are other costs for the justice system. The process of convicting offenders and then sending people to jail is very expensive. Healthcare costs in providing treatment for drug users are also high. The biggest cost to the wider economy is from a decrease in productivity. That is because people are unable to work or lose their jobs because of their drug problems, trouble with the justice system, or serious health problems. Many employers drug-test their workers, due to safety concerns. This may also mean they have to find new staff if employees test positive for drugs.

## Racial Inequality

One of the biggest criticisms of the war on drugs is that it has worsened racial inequality in the United States. One adviser to President Nixon claimed that the war on drugs was deliberately designed to target Black communities. When tougher sentences for drug possession were introduced in the 1980s, opponents argued that these were also designed to discriminate against people of color. The law gave tougher sentences for possessing a small quantity of crack cocaine, which was more common in Black neighborhoods, than drugs that were more likely to be used by white people. There was also evidence that Black offenders were given longer prison terms than white offenders.

## Targeting Black Americans

Even now, when marijuana has been decriminalized in many states, Black Americans are still more likely to be arrested for possessing the drug. This unequal approach to enforcing drug laws is one reason why Black Americans are more than five times as likely to be in jail as white Americans. Gun violence is often linked to drug supply, and Black Americans are far more likely to be killed or injured by gun violence.

## Ethnic Groups Treated Unequally

At one time, it seemed that the opioid crisis sweeping the United States was following a pattern that was different from that of other illegal drugs. Overdoses from opioids, which often resulted from the use of prescription medicines, affected older white Americans more than other groups. Yet, this pattern changed as opioid overdose increased among Black Americans. Black and Hispanic Americans are also more likely than white people to be convicted for trafficking the synthetic opioid fentanyl.

The rising threat of drug overdose is a major problem for healthcare as well as law enforcement.

## Gang Warfare

Opponents of the war on drugs argue that it gives more power to criminal gangs. Criminals have created highly organized gangs to transport drugs from where they are produced, often in Asia or South America, to cities around the world. These gangs make more money than most legal businesses. They use fear and violence to protect themselves and stay ahead of their competitors. Well-armed and ruthless gangs are more likely to be successful in this trade. The huge profits they make are used to fund other criminal activities. This then further increases the risk of crime across society.

Legal drugs, such as opium used in medicine for pain relief, often come from the same plants and locations as illegal drugs but do not have the same violence associated with them. This shows that the gangs and violence happen because of the illegal trade and efforts of governments to stop it.

## Mexico's Drug War

In some cases, the effects of drug wars elsewhere in the world have been even more devastating. In Mexico, the government war against drug cartels costs thousands of lives every year. Politicians, journalists, and innocent people have been caught up in a brutal war that they didn't start.

Armed forces in Mexico are engaged in a difficult ongoing battle against drug cartels.

Drug gangs have no interest in protecting the environment and build bases deep in the rain forest to stay hidden.

The United States has spent billions of dollars supporting the Mexican government in this war to try and stop the supply of drugs from Mexico.

During conflicts between governments and drug cartels, laws are often broken on both sides. Suspected drug traffickers may be assassinated or locked up without a trial. In many countries, those who are found to be carrying small amounts of drugs may face long prison sentences or even execution.

Sometimes these drug wars are successful in capturing key figures in the drug trade. However, as long as the trade continues and there is demand for drugs, someone else will soon take over from the captured gang leader.

## The Impact on the Environment

Like many other industries, the global trade in drugs has an environmental impact. Environmental campaigners have pointed out that the war on drugs is driving drug traffickers deep into the rain forests of Central America. There, they build airstrips, roads, and clear areas for farming. This destroys vital habitats for animals and plants. Campaigners argue that it would be more effective to spend money supporting poorer communities and the environment rather than trying to defeat the drug traffickers.

# 21ST CENTURY DEBATES

# Do Drug Wars Increase Racial Inequality?

Racial inequality is a major issue in the United States. People of color, and particularly Black Americans, have less wealth than white Americans. They also usually have poorer health and lower graduation rates. Critics of the war on drugs argue that it has made many of these issues worse because laws and the police have targeted people of color more than other groups. Others disagree. Here are the two opposing viewpoints.

## Drug Wars Worsen Racial Inequality

People argue that the war on drugs is making racial inequality worse for the following reasons:

**Impact on Black and minority people:** Figures show that Black Americans and other minorities are much more likely than white people to be arrested. They are also five times more likely to go to jail for drug offenses.

**Laws tougher on some drugs:** Laws from the 1980s gave tougher penalties for possessing quantities of drugs that were more likely to be used in poorer neighborhoods with larger Black populations than drugs traditionally used by wealthier white drug users. These laws have been changed but still do not treat drug offenses equally.

**Violent crime:** Much of the violent crime associated with drug gangs is more likely to affect neighborhoods with large Black populations. And young Black men are more likely to be victims of gun crime or police shootings than any other group.

## Conclusion

Attempts to crack down on drug use have had a particular impact on Black communities. In some cases, laws have been designed to target drug use in Black communities. Violent crime linked to drug gangs also has a big impact on the lives of Black American communities.

## Drug Wars Do Not Increase Racial Inequality

Opponents of the view that drug wars add to the problem of racial inequality argue that it cannot be blamed on drug policy for the following reasons:

**Racial inequality is not new:** Racial inequality has been going on for hundreds of years in the United States, long before the war on drugs. More Black Americans live in poorer neighborhoods where drugs are more of a problem. This is the real reason for racial inequality.

**Laws apply to all:** Laws are the same for all members of the community. If some groups are convicted of more drug crimes, this is because they are either using or supplying illegal drugs.

**Gun crime is not linked solely to illegal drugs:** Gun-related violence can be linked to many different things, including easy access to gun ownership. Drugs may make it worse, but gun crime would exist in Black communities even if drugs were not a problem.

## Conclusion

The higher rates of drug offenses and incarceration in particular communities happen because of the inequality that already exists in society. It does not make it worse. There are many reasons for racial inequality—it is not all down to drugs.

## What Do You Think?

After reading both sides of the argument, what conclusions do you draw? Do you agree with those who say that the war on drugs has made inequality worse? Or do you think higher levels of drug use and related crime are caused by the inequalities in our society?

Chapter 5

# Tackling Drug Wars

Since the 1970s, the US Government has used two main ways to try to deal with drug abuse. The first is tough penalties to stop people taking drugs. The second is trying to stop illegal drugs reaching the United States. Both methods have cost many billions of dollars and increased the prison population across the country. However, it could be argued that despite these efforts, today, illegal drugs are a bigger problem than ever. What other options are there to deal with this problem?

## Treatment for Addicts

Addiction is one of the main reasons why there is such demand for illegal drugs. During the opioid crisis that has cost so many lives, many people began taking legal drugs for pain relief. But they then turned to illegal sources to feed their addiction. Treatment has been downplayed since the war on drugs was launched, with treatment for addiction often only offered as part of a jail term. Experts argue that far more funding should be given to treating drug users and that taking this approach will reduce the demand for drugs.

This campaigner is calling on the president to do more about the opioid crisis that has caused so many deaths.

## Making Drugs Safer

Drug abuse involves huge health risks. There is currently no reliable way for drug users to know what is mixed in with the drugs they take or how strong they are. This raises the risk of a fatal overdose. Overdoses have increased with the spread of powerful synthetic opioids. These dangerous substances may be added to other drugs.

Health experts argue that the best way to reduce overdoses is to give drug users access to testing and supervised places for injecting drugs. This would enable people to have a better understanding of what drugs contain, and their likely effects. It would also stop the spread of infections from sharing or using dirty needles. Tests have found that these facilities, which have been tried in many countries, also reduce drug-related crime.

**Supporters of decriminalizing marijuana argue that a legal drug is easier to control and people can be protected from negative effects.**

## Decriminalizing Drugs

Mandatory prison sentences for drug possession have led to a big rise in the number of nonviolent prisoners for drug-related crimes. It is very expensive and has other negative effects on the lives of minor offenders.

The most widely used illegal drug in the United States is marijuana, and many states have now taken the decision to decriminalize this drug or make possession of small amounts legal. In 2021, Oregon became the first state to decriminalize possession of small amounts of any drug. Decriminalizing some drugs helps reduce the pressure on prisons by reducing the numbers of people locked up for using drugs. Police resources can then be used to target the supply of dangerous illegal drugs. If drug users are less worried about facing prison for using drugs, they may be more likely to seek help for addiction and other health issues.

**Would decriminalizing drugs reduce trafficking and the violence that goes with it?**

## Negative Effects of Decriminalization

Many health professionals argue for a more humane approach to illegal drugs, treating them as a public health issue. However, other people argue that this is not the right approach. Opponents of decriminalizing drugs believe that doing this will lead to an epidemic of drug addiction as people no longer fear going to prison for minor drug offenses.

This growth in addiction could put extra pressure on health and treatment services and also increase other negative effects, such as crime to pay for drugs. It could mean drug users are tempted by stronger and more harmful drugs. Results from drug policies in Portugal and elsewhere suggest that these fears may not be fully justified, but further research is needed.

## The Continuing War on the Drug Trade

Supporters of the war on drugs argue that lack of success in some areas is not a reason to abandon the approach altogether. Illegal drugs still cause a lot of harm. Even if possession of some drugs is made legal, much of the supply of these drugs will be controlled by criminal gangs. That means much of the crime and violence associated with the drug trade will continue. If marijuana is legalized, gangs may simply switch to focus on even more dangerous and addictive drugs that are still illegal.

People who think it is important to stop the supply of illegal drugs argue that the government should focus on breaking up organized crime to reduce trafficking, rather than incarcerating drug users. Criminal gangs are responsible for widespread violence and other areas of criminal activity. Stopping the gangs means working closely with police and government in other countries. As well as trying to stay one step ahead of criminal gangs, investing in countries most badly affected by the drug trade could give new opportunities to local people who are not controlled by the gangs.

## The Portugal Model

Portugal in the European Union (EU) has taken an approach to tackling drug addiction that is different from many other countries. During the 1990s, Portugal was home to around 100,000 heroin addicts. Rates of HIV infection were high, and half the prison population was linked to drug-related crime. Portugal switched from waging a war on drugs to treating drug addicts. By 2023, Portugal's number of heroin users was reduced to 25,000 and drug use is below the European average.

Growing coca plants is attractive because profits are so high. Only cutting demand for the drug will change this.

# 21ST CENTURY DEBATES

## Has the War on Drugs Failed?

After more than 50 years, many organizations and experts agree that the war on drugs has been a failure. Illegal drugs are more of a problem in the present than they were when this war was launched. Experts argue that the war itself has had negative effects. However, there are still many people who believe that the war on drugs should be fought and can make a difference. Let's take a look at both sides of the debate.

## The War Has Been Lost

People argue that the war on drugs has failed for the following reasons:

**Soaring numbers of drug overdoses:** The purpose of the war on drugs is to protect people and communities from the harmful effects of drugs. Why then have drug overdoses been rising in recent decades? These surges in overdoses prove that the war on drugs has failed.

**Negative effects of mandatory sentences:** One of the main effects of the war on drugs has been to increase the number of minor offenders in prison. However, it has not stopped the supply of drugs into US towns and cities. This policy has also increased racial inequality.

**Failing to stop the drug trade:** The war on drugs has focused on drug users solely in the United States. It has not done enough to tackle international drug trade. International drug cartels have simply become more violent and powerful in response to the war against them.

## Conclusion

In many ways, the problem of illegal drugs and related violence in the United States is worse today than it ever has been in our history. We now have more drug overdoses and more people in jail than ever before. There are few obvious achievements as a result of the drugs war. Looking at this evidence, the conclusion is that the war failed.

## The War Had to Be Fought

Supporters of the war on drugs argue that it is still worthwhile for the following reasons:

**Attacking the dangers of drugs:** Tough measures for both using or supplying illegal drugs make it clear to the public that drugs are a major health issue. That deters many people from abusing illegal drugs.

**Hard to measure the effects:** The use of illegal drugs is still high, but it is difficult to measure what would have happened to illegal drug use without the war on drugs. The epidemic of drug use and the effects on communities could have been even more serious than it is.

**It was an unavoidable war:** Some of the tactics used in the war on drugs have been less successful than planned. However, it was not an option to simply ignore the drugs problem and the damage they do to our communities.

## Conclusion

Before we conclude that the war on drugs has failed, we should ask what would have happened if strict measures had not been taken to control illegal drugs. They may have had an even worse effect on our society and more people would today be ignorant of the dangers of drugs. Something had to be done to deal with the illegal supply and use of drugs in order to protect society.

## What Do You Think?

After reading both sides of the argument, what conclusions do you draw? Do you think that the war on drugs has been a waste of time and resources? Or do you think a tough approach to illegal drugs was needed and the war has had some success?

Chapter 6

# Solutions to Drug Wars

People have been using legal and illegal drugs for thousands of years. Attempts to stop this by declaring war on drugs have not solved the problem. So, has anything worked to reduce the harmful effects of drugs, and what plans could work in future?

## Changing Attitudes

Surveys show that Americans are less concerned about illegal drugs than they are about some other issues, including crime. This shows that attitudes are changing and people recognize the need for new solutions to illegal drug use. Eight out of 10 Americans say the war on drugs has failed and support ending the war. These changing attitudes show that people would support different approaches to problems caused by illegal drugs.

Trying to fight a military war against drugs has led to thousands of deaths in Mexico.

Synthetic drugs present new problems for health professionals

## An Evolving Problem

The issues around illegal drugs have also changed. The growing problem of powerful synthetic opioid drugs such as fentanyl means new challenges for health professionals and law enforcement. This drug is present in two-thirds of drug overdose deaths. Fentanyl is mixed with other drugs by drug cartels to cut their costs. This severe health risk makes it all the more important that support is provided to stop accidental overdoses.

## Future Solutions

Opponents of the current war on drugs believe governments should accept that a drug-free society is not possible. This will clear the way to educate people about the risks and provide better treatment and support, such as testing of drugs. A more open approach to drugs could also enable more research into the causes of drug abuse.

Any long-term solution to the issue needs to address some of the harm caused by prison sentences for drug offenses. As we have seen, these sentences are more likely to affect poorer groups in society and people of color. In addition to the prison terms, employers discriminate against people with drug offenses so it is more difficult for them to find a job. Looking at drug abuse as a health problem may help to deal with this prejudice.

## Stopping the Supply

Ending the supply of illegal drugs and defeating the drug cartels is another major issue. However, taking a more varied and health-based approach could reduce the demand for drugs and therefore the riches available to the cartels. Some experts argue that governments could do more to seize the billions of dollars in profits made by these gangs. Lasting solutions will require cooperation around the world.

# 21ST CENTURY DEBATES

## Can Anyone Win the War on Drugs?

After more than 50 years, many experts have concluded that the US Government's war on drugs has failed. The search for solutions to the issue of illegal drugs and crime goes on. Is it possible to end the problems caused by the illegal drugs trade? Some people believe so, but others think it is a battle we cannot win. Let's look at both viewpoints.

## An Unwinnable War

People believe that we will never stop the negative effects of illegal drugs for the following reasons:

**Drug-free society is not possible:** All attempts to stop illegal drugs have failed so far. Whatever laws are passed, there will always be a demand for drugs and someone will always supply that demand.

**Criminalizing drugs has not worked:** The main idea behind criminalizing even minor drug offenses was to make it too risky for people to use illegal drugs. However, addiction and other reasons that people use drugs mean that some individuals will always take the risk.

**Global supply of drugs:** The drug trade is a huge global business—one that is bigger than any country can control. Criminal gangs will take on governments because the riches available are so great. They will simply ignore the effect on others.

## Conclusion

No country has ever been able to stop illegal drugs completely, and the huge resources used in the war on drugs have failed to achieve this. Other approaches may be more successful, but the illegal trade in drugs will never be completely defeated. The forces that drive illegal drug supply and use are just too great to overcome. It is impossible for a country to do that.

## A Different Approach Could Work

Others are more optimistic about the prospects of winning this war for the following reasons:

**Setting goals:** It may not be possible to end all use of illegal drugs, but governments could set clearer goals to reduce the harm that drugs do. Those goals could include ending drug-related crime or better supporting drug users so they quit.

**Healthcare solutions:** The war on drugs has treated drug abuse as a crime. Treating this as a public health issue has been shown to work in some places and can deal with some of the harmful effects of drugs.

**Global solutions:** It is difficult for one country to solve the problem. However, countries have shown they can work together to solve global problems in the past. They could work together in the same way to provide a solution to drug wars around the world.

## Conclusion

What do we mean by winning the war on drugs? If we really want to stop people dying and the many other negative effects of drugs, that could be achieved with treatment. Global cooperation is needed to end the global drug trade. If countries start working together, they will be a force that has enough power to really deal with drugs and the damage that they cause.

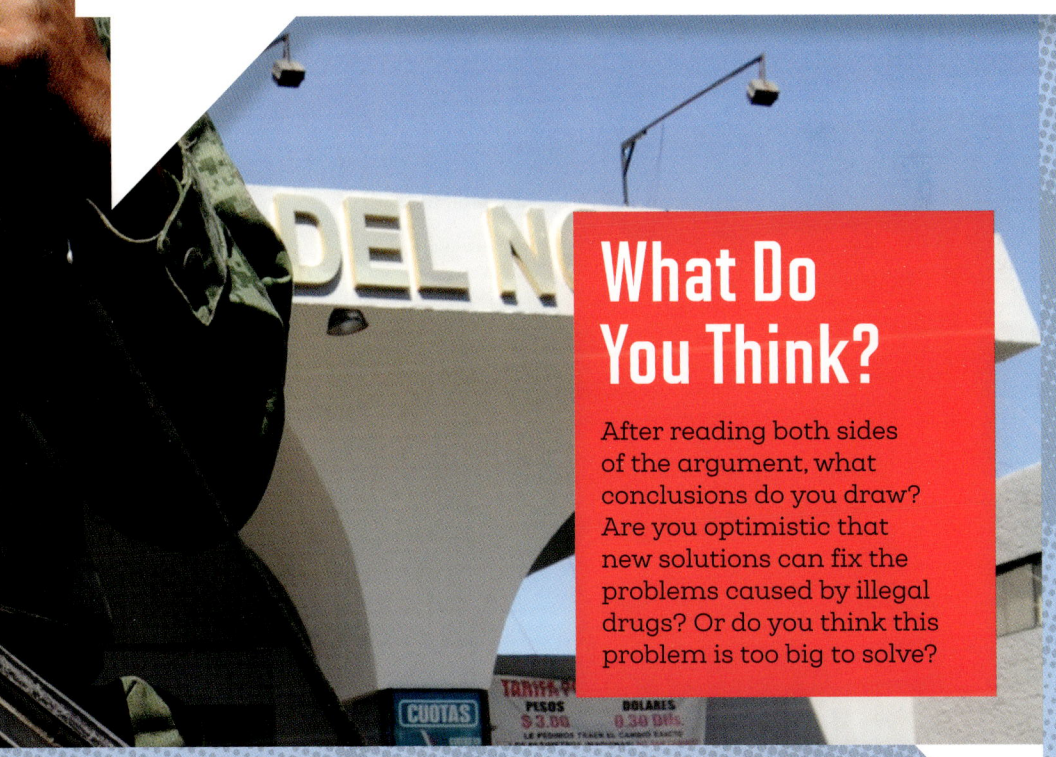

## What Do You Think?

After reading both sides of the argument, what conclusions do you draw? Are you optimistic that new solutions can fix the problems caused by illegal drugs? Or do you think this problem is too big to solve?

## Looking for Solutions

Even as deaths from drug overdoses climbed in recent years, surveys have found that drug addiction is less of a concern for Americans than it has been in the past. A majority of Americans also feel that marijuana should be legal. These results could suggest that most Americans feel that a different approach should be taken to illegal drugs.

Try to think about how your own life and the lives of people you know have been affected by drugs and related issues, or could be in the future. Consider your own attitudes to some of the questions raised in this book, for example:

- Why are illegal drugs such a major health issue in the United States?
- Have drugs and related issues affected your family or people you know?
- What other effects has drug abuse had in your local area, such as crime?
- What would be the most effective ways to deal with illegal drugs?

## Questions for Us All

Looking for answers to questions like those above will help you understand the issues around illegal drugs and drug wars and how they affect your community. By understanding the debates around drug wars, we will have a better understanding of why they are such difficult problems to address. If we all do that, we may be able to better solve some of the questions around this twenty-first century issue.

A protester illustrates some of the many lives lost to the opioid crisis.

# Find Out More

## Books

Eason, Sarah and Karen Latchana Kenney. *Having a Drug Addiction: Stories from Survivors* (It Happened to Me). Cheriton Children's Books, 2022.

Quinones, Sam. *Dreamland: The True Story of America's Opiate Epidemic* (YA Edition). Bloomsbury, 2019.

Scheff, David and Nic. *High: Everything You Want to Know About Drugs, Alcohol, and Addiction*. Clarion Books, 2019.

Smith, Elliott. *The Opioid Epidemic and the Addiction Crisis*. Lerner Publishing Group, 2022.

## Websites

KidsHealth is one of many websites that provide factual information on drugs and related issues:
**https://kidshealth.org/en/kids/know-drugs.html**

Discover more about the debate surrounding legalizing marijuana at:
**https://marijuana.procon.org**

This video from CNBC looks looking at issues around the war on drugs:
**http://youtu.be/LXmtsIYsYjY?feature=shared**

**Publisher's note to educators and parents:**
All the websites featured above have been carefully reviewed to ensure that they are suitable for students. However, many websites change often, and we cannot guarantee that a site's future contents will continue to meet our high standards of educational value. Please be advised that students should be closely monitored whenever they access the Internet.

# Glossary

**addiction** a physical or psychological need for a particular substance that the addicted person is unable to easily control

**assassinated** murdered a specific or important person, often for political reasons

**cocaine** a type of drug manufactured from the leaves of the coca plant, which mainly grows in South America

**competitor** a person or business that is competing with or trying to gain advantage over another

**crack cocaine** a powerful and highly addictive form of cocaine

**decriminalize** to remove the criminal status of something, such as possession of a drug

**dependent** relying on something or addicted to it

**deterrent** something designed to stop people from doing something, for example, prison is a deterrent to stop drug abuse

**discriminate** to treat a person or group of people unfairly, especially if this is due to race, religion, gender, or disability

**drug cartels** criminal organizations made up of separate gangs that work together to organize the production and trafficking of drugs

**Drug Enforcement Agency (DEA)** an agency set up by President Nixon to pursue the war on drugs

**enforcement** the act of giving force or enforcing something, such as the law

**epidemic** an illness or problem that affects a large number of people

**fatal** describing something that leads to death

**Federal** relating to the overall government of the United States, rather than an individual state

**fentanyl** a powerful synthetic opioid drug, which has been blamed for an increased number of drug overdoses

**HIV** human immunodeficiency virus, which damages the immune system and causes the disease AIDS

**homicide** the killing of one person by another

**humane** showing compassion or empathy for others

**incarcerate** to put in prison

**ineffective** not effective or not achieving an intended outcome

**inequality** when something is unequal, such as inequality between certain groups of people in society

**infection** a disease or illness caused by a bacteria or virus

**infectious** describes an illness that can be passed from one person to another

**justice system** the system a society uses to enforce laws, including courts and prisons

**majority** the greater part or more than half of something

**mandatory** compulsory or required

**marijuana** a drug that is produced from parts of the hemp plant

**minority** describes the smaller part of something, such as a group of people in the population who are not the majority

**opioid** a natural or synthetic drug that affects the body in the same way as drugs that are produced from the opium poppy

**opium** a drug produced from the opium poppy

**organized crime** an organization or gang that exists to carry out crimes on a large scale, such as trafficking in drugs

**overdose** a toxic amount of a drug that can lead to serious health problems or death

**people trafficking** smuggling people across national borders as illegal immigrants

**prejudice** bias or negative feelings toward a person or group of people

**prescribes** authorizes something as a cure for an illness or condition, such as when a doctor prescribes a particular drug

**prescription drugs** drugs that are legal and available through a prescription from a doctor

**racial inequality** unequal status between different races or ethnic groups in society

**regulate** to introduce and follow rules to manage something

**sentence** a punishment given by a court, such as a period of time in prison

**smugglers** people who move something in secret or illegally to avoid discovery by authorities

**synthetic** made by humans or chemical process rather than by natural means

**synthetic opioid** an opioid drug made by a chemical process rather than being produced from opium poppy

**traffickers** people who transport something, often illegally across borders

**unemployment** the state of not having a job

**vulnerable** at risk of harm

# Index

addiction 4, 6–7, 11–12, 16, 18, 20–22, 24, 27, 34–37, 42, 44–45
Afghanistan 4, 8–9

Black Americans 13, 25, 29, 32–33

Canada 21
cannabis 6–7
Caribbean 15
Central America 4, 9, 15, 31
cocaine 7, 12–15, 28
Colombia 4
crack cocaine 12–13, 28
crime and drugs 5–6, 9, 13–14, 16–17, 20, 22–24, 27, 30, 32–33, 35–37, 40, 42–44

decriminalization 36
demand for drugs 10–12, 14, 16, 31, 34, 37, 41–42
disease and drugs 7, 19, 23
drug cartels 4, 15, 23, 30–31, 38, 41
drug dealers 14
Drug Enforcement Agency (DEA) 13
drug-related deaths 7, 13, 19, 21, 26, 34, 40–41, 44
drug producers 8, 15
drug use and drug users 4–5, 10, 13, 16, 18–19, 22–24, 32–33, 37, 39–40

fentanyl 7, 19, 21, 29, 41

gangs and drugs 4, 9, 14–15, 23–25, 30–32, 36–37, 41–42
government 5, 8–15, 26, 28, 30–31, 34, 37, 41–43

heroin 7–8, 19, 37
homicides 9, 15, 23–25

illegal drugs 4–10, 14–16, 18–25, 29, 33–40, 42–44

justice system 26, 28

laws about drugs 13, 29, 31–33, 42
legal drugs 21, 30, 34–35

marijuana 6–7, 12, 23, 27, 29, 35–36, 44–45
mental health issues 7
methamphetamine (crystal meth) 7
Mexico 4, 15, 30–31, 40

opioids 5, 7, 13, 19, 21–22, 24, 29, 34–35, 41, 44–45
organized crime 9, 37
overdoses 4, 7, 13, 19, 21, 24, 26, 29, 35, 38, 41, 44

Portugal 36–37
prescription drugs 8
prison 5, 8, 13–14, 16–17, 20, 22, 24, 27–28, 31, 34–38, 41

racial inequality and drugs 23, 28, 32–33, 38

synthetic drugs 7–8, 41

traffickers 8, 10–12, 15, 23, 31
trafficking routes 15, 25
treating drug addicts 17, 37

unemployment and drugs 18, 22–24
United States 4–6, 8–10, 13–16, 19, 21, 23–29, 31–35, 38, 44

violence and drugs 6, 14, 16–17, 23–25, 29–30, 33, 36–38

## About the Author

Nick Hunter is a well-known children's book author who has written books on a huge range of subjects, from history and science through politics and geography. Researching and writing this book has made him even more aware of the complex issues surrounding drug wars, the risk they pose to our society, and the urgent need to address this twenty-first century problem.